ENDORSEMENT

Jordan Rogers presents in this short book a concise treatise on salvation and our response to the grace and mercy that comes only from a true relationship with Jesus Christ. It is a must read for any church member who struggles with their own eternal hope for salvation. It will be one of those books I read multiple times throughout the years of my life to remind myself of what Jesus has done for me.

Eric Roberts, Worship Pastor,
Hillcrest Baptist Church of Nederland, TX

Authentic Faith

JORDAN ROGERS

LUCIDBOOKS

Authentic Faith

Published by Lucid Books in Houston, TX.
www.LucidBooks.net

First Printing 2015

ISBN-13: 978-1-63296-031-3
ISBN-10: 1632960311

eISBN 10: 163296032X
eISBN 13: 978-1-63296-032-0

Special Sales: Most Lucid Books titles are available in special quantity discounts. Custom imprinting or excerpting can also be done to fit special needs. Contact Lucid Books at info@lucidbooks.net.

TABLE OF CONTENTS

FOREWORD

IT IS WITH wholehearted approval that I recommend *Authentic Faith* to you. Jordan skillfully incorporates the scriptures into his work and writes with the heart of a pastor. A work like this is as relevant as ever in our postmodern world. Jordan encourages us to *Examine Our Faith* and reminds us that a *Saving Faith is a Living Faith*. Frankly speaking, Jesus should make a radical difference in our lives. In my lifetime, John MacArthur created a firestorm of controversy by addressing the subject of true faith and how it relates to Christ's lordship.

False promises of an easy life or indulgence of sins. But in good times, the cost does not seem so high, and people take the name of Christ without undergoing the radical transformation of life that true conversion implies.

John F. MacArthur Jr. The Gospel According to Jesus: What Is Authentic Faith?

AUTHENTIC FAITH

What passes off for real faith (in Christ) today is a far cry from the "faith of our fathers." Jordan reminds the church of a long forgotten facet of salvation's message in *Saving Faith is Repentant Faith*. I am oft amused when I hear people say, "We need to make Jesus Lord!" How can we add something to him that God already gave him? "Let all the house of Israel therefore know for certain that God has made him both Lord and Christ, this Jesus whom you crucified (Acts 2:36)." We do not make him Lord; he is lord! Moreover, that same Lord makes us a new creation and Jordan displays this convincingly in the *Fruit of Saving Faith*, a tonic for easy believism.

> Cheap grace is the grace we bestow on ourselves. Cheap grace is the preaching of forgiveness without requiring repentance, baptism without church discipline, communion without confession. Cheap grace is grace without discipleship, grace without the cross, grace without Jesus Christ, living and incarnate. Costly grace...is the kingly rule of Christ, for whose sake a man will pluck out the eye which causes him to stumble, it is the call of Jesus Christ at which the disciple leaves his nets and follows him.
>
> ***Dietrich Bonhoeffer***
> ***The Cost of Discipleship***

One cannot ignore personal faith, for the stakes are eternal and the souls of men hang-in-the-balance. Many professing Christians live with complete disregard for the commands of Christ – for them, they are still under the wrath of God. In *Saving Faith Endures*, Jordan helps us to see that perseverance is an integral part of God's salvific work in us. He makes the singular command to the church, "make disciples" extremely practical in the chapter *Discipleship*. In *Keeping the Gospel Difficult* gets to the crux of how to keep salvation real, genuine, and potent. The words of our Lord still ring true and poignant.

> "Not everyone who says to me, 'Lord, Lord,' will enter the kingdom of heaven, but the one who does the will of my Father who is in heaven. On that day many will say to me, 'Lord, Lord, did we not prophesy in your name, and cast out demons in your name, and do many mighty works in your name?' And then will I declare to them, 'I never knew you; depart from me, you workers of lawlessness.'

> **Jesus Christ**
> **Matthew 7:21-23**

Jordan has done a service to his God and the church through *Authentic Faith*. I pray that it will serve as a blessing to the Christian and cause them to rejoice that God can genuinely save to the uttermost. Likewise, I pray that it will serve as a source of conviction, prompting the lost to realize what authentic faith really is- a life radically changed by the Gospel, that the whole world can see.

Proud Dad
Blessed Mentor
Co-laborer with Christ

Tony A. Rogers
Bowie, Texas

CHAPTER 1

5 Reasons to Examine Your Faith

WHY IS IT so important to test the authenticity of your faith in God? Let me convince you of this need, if you are not already, by giving you five reasons you ought to examine your faith. This book is written for the express purpose of helping you examine whether or not your "faith" in God is legitimate according to the Bible. Allow me clarify: when I write the term "authentic faith", what I mean is *Biblically* authentic. That is, faith according to Scripture. The fact is that we are all in need of testing our belief and *Who* we are putting our hope in for this life and eternity.

(1) You are justified (saved) by faith.

The Bible teaches us that a person is justified by faith. Now, I will take the time to explain what I mean by saying "justified by faith" so that we can avoid confusion. Justification is a legal term. It means that a person is considered righteous, or guiltless; that is, *in good standing*. When the Bible speaks of justification, it is speaking about our being considered righteous by God, or *in good standing*.

Scripture teaches us that God declares a person righteous through their faith. Romans 3:28 says, "For we hold that one is justified by faith apart from works of the law." This is absolutely crucial! The Bible tells us that God declares a person righteous, not because of their deeds, but because of their faith. I want you to understand the importance of this, because if a person was only considered righteous because of their deeds, everyone would be considered sinful and guilty. Romans 3:10 says, "None is righteous, no, not one" and Romans 3:23 says, "all have sinned and fall short of the glory of God." If faith is the only way we are to be considered righteous in God's eyes, then we better get faith right because "the unrighteous will not inherit the kingdom of God" (1 Corinthians 6:9)[1].

How is God able to declare a sinner righteous and remain just? We know that "the wages of sin is death" (Romans 6:23), and that fine must be paid. This is where the good news comes in: God sent His only Son, Jesus Christ, into this world to live a perfect life and then die the death that we deserve so that He would be able to forgive us our sin and consider our penalty paid. In this way God is able "to be just and the justifier of the one who has faith in Jesus" (Romans 3:26).

This is why knowing that your faith is genuine is so incredibly important! If we are forgiven according to our faith, then we must strive with all our effort to know that our

---

1   The *English Standard Version* (ESV) will used throughout when Scripture is referenced.

faith is correct. That brings us to the second reason we should examine our faith.

(2) The consequence of false faith is infinitely severe and final.

If the Bible tells us what saving faith is, and we don't have *that* faith, then there are dire consequences. Look at a passage of Scripture with me.

Matthew 7:21-23 says, "²¹Not everyone who says to Me, 'Lord, Lord,' will enter the kingdom of heaven, but the one who does the will of My Father who is in heaven. ²²On that day many will say to Me, 'Lord, Lord, did we not prophesy in Your name, and cast out demons in Your name, and do many works in Your name?' ²³And then I will declare to them, 'I never knew you; depart from Me, you workers of lawlessness.'"

Why is it so important that we know if our faith (our belief and commitment to Christ) is Biblically genuine? Notice the consequence in vs.23, "depart from Me, you workers of lawlessness." The consequence of having a false faith is severe to the uttermost. Notice Jesus calls these people, "workers of lawlessness." This is because apart from Biblical faith, a person is not forgiven by God but is rather considered unrighteous—a worker of lawlessness.

When Jesus says, "depart from Me", the fact that you are separated from your Creator and all His grace is bad enough, but the reality is that the Bible teaches us that you are separated *forever*—for eternity in a place called Hell. Jesus teaches us about Hell in Matthew 25:41 which says, "⁴¹Then

He will say to those on His left, 'Depart from Me, you cursed, into the eternal fire prepared for the devil and his angels….'" and vs.46 which says, "⁴⁶And these will go away into eternal punishment, but the righteous into eternal life." Hell is eternal. The punishment for sin is everlasting.

The punishment is everlasting and the judgment for sin is final and irreversible upon death. Hebrews 9:27 says, "it is appointed for man to die once, and after that comes judgment." There are no "do overs" when you die. There is no opportunity at that point to make things right between yourself and your Maker. Therefore, it is crucial that you examine yourself now! Apart from Biblical faith, the consequence for sin is catastrophic.

In my opinion, there does not necessarily need to be any other reasons for asking yourself if your faith is authentic, because the reasons already presented are convincing enough. However, there are more reasons, which brings us to number three.

(3) There is a kind of faith that is not unto salvation.

I have already used the term *authentic faith*, and by using that term I am implying that there is an inauthentic or fraudulent and false faith. What I mean is that there is a kind of faith that is not unto salvation. Jesus talked about this very thing, that there are people in this world who believe that they are right with God, but they are deceiving themselves. Upon entering into eternity (upon death) they will be shocked to find that their faith was not Biblically authentic and thus it was not effective to save them. Let's look again at Jesus' teaching on this in Matthew 7:22-23:

"²²On that day many will say to Me, 'Lord, Lord, did we not prophesy in Your name, and cast out demons in Your name, and do many works in Your name?' ²³And then I will declare to them, 'I never knew you; depart from Me, you workers of lawlessness.'"

There are many things that are amazing in this text. Take notice of the confession of the people who are sent away to Hell in this instance. They say, "Lord, Lord" to Jesus, yet He does not know them. Immediately you realize that there is something going on here that is strange. Why are these people who call Jesus "Lord" sent to Hell? Some people might say, "I thought that was all I had to do was acknowledge Jesus was Lord!" Evidently, that is not the Biblical definition of saving faith. Some, or rather *many* people, possess a counterfeit faith.

There is a kind of faith, even a *Christian-like* faith that is not unto salvation. In many churches a person who walks to the front after a service to pray with the pastor and then says that they acknowledge Jesus as Lord is recognized as a "believer" and is then baptized. However, according to Matthew 7 there are many people who call Jesus "Lord" but do not truly know Him in the saving way. Though these people may be considered "Christian" in our culture, sadly, many of them are not truly Christians. This is why I said that there is a kind of faith, even a *Christian-like* faith that is not unto salvation. Notice how deep the deception is as well. These people begin to claim to have done many marvelous deeds in the name of Christ Jesus, but those claims do not change their fate. These people who are turned away from Heaven many times *appear* to be Christian because they hold to Christian morals and they fit into church crowds.

Being a moral person does not mean that you have *saving*

faith. Many people are confused by their good morals, thinking that because they are *ethical* and *principled*, they should be considered Christian. However, while their life may be moral in a sense, they are lacking obedience to the things that Christ commands in Scripture and have never truly been *born again* (John 3:1-21). The Pharisees were the religious leaders of Israel in the days of Jesus. They were the keepers of the Scriptures and the teachers in the synagogues. They were so strict about keeping the Law and being *moral* that non-Pharisees could not even compare. However, Jesus had His harshest criticisms reserved for these religious people. They seemed to be moral people, but only in appearance. They spent all of their time and energy to present themselves as *clean* and moral, but they passed over the fact that righteousness before God is only gained by faith in Him. They were masters of appearances, but they were neglectful of the heart and lacking in true faith. Take for instance the words of Jesus to the Pharisees in Luke 11:39-41, "[39]And the Lord said to him, "Now you Pharisees cleanse the outside of the cup and of the dish, but inside you are full of greed and wickedness. [40]You fools! Did not He who made the outside make the inside also? [41]But give as alms those things that are within, and behold, everything is clean for you."

The Pharisees certainly believed that God considered them righteous and that therefore they were "saved", but their righteousness was only in appearance. Many people who fall into this category of believing they are saved when they are not, fail here because they are ignorant of what the Bible says about what real, authentic, saving faith is and how it manifests itself in a person. To find if this is true one only needs to ask, "Can you tell me what the Bible says a true follower of Christ receives from God when they are saved and can you tell me what their life ought to look like in terms of belief and action?" Tragically, many people who attend churches today cannot answer that question because they are ignorant of what the Bible actually teaches about what saving faith really is. This is why the pews of churches are populated by a great number of people who will be turned away from Heaven because they never knew Jesus.

The Apostle John writes this of false believers in 1 John 2:19, "¹⁹They went out from us, but they were not of us; for if they had been of us, they would have continued with us. But they went out, that it might become plain that they all are not of us." We will come back to this passage later on in the book when we look at the persevering nature of true faith, but I want you to notice something that John says here. These *false Christians* went out *from their midst*. The false believers were not found in the bars and streets. No, they were found in the midst of true believers as he says, "They went out from us, but they were not of us." There are people in the midst of churches that are moral, have good attendance, and seem to have it together, but they do not know Christ. They do not possess saving faith.

Another passage that we will come back to is Matthew 13:24-30, 36-43 which is Jesus teaching the parable of the weeds among the wheat. In this parable Jesus tells us that the wheat represents the people who know Jesus and will inherit Heaven, and the weeds are the people who will not inherit Heaven. The shocking thing that He teaches us in this is that the weeds grow up right next to the wheat. Now, I have lived in places where there are many wheat farmers, and they will tell you that there is a plant that grows among the wheat that is called "tares" or "darnel." Many refer to this plant as "false wheat" because it so resembles the wheat and the only time you can tell they difference is when the harvest comes. That is precisely the lesson Jesus teaches here, that there are false Christians who grow up right next to authentic Christians and they are so similar in way that if you don't really know what you're looking for—you can't tell the difference.

A discerning eye, the eye of an experienced farmer, can tell the difference between false wheat and genuine wheat (we will talk about this in greater detail later on). The farmer keeps the wheat during the harvest; the weeds are discarded and destroyed. A man that is ignorant of wheat's true properties is left to his ignorance until the harvest. Helpless also is a person who is ignorant of the Bible's description of what genuine faith in Christ is until the day he stands before His Creator to be judged. Therefore, it is so important for you and I to examine what the Bible says that saving faith is so that we know without a doubt that we have come to know Christ in the saving way.

This brings us to the fourth reason we should examine our faith.

(4) There are "many" who possess a counterfeit faith.

Notice that in vs.22 of Matthew 7 Jesus said that there will be "many" who claim to have known Him only to be greeted with that eternal judgment, "I never knew you; depart from Me, you workers of lawlessness." That is a haunting statement.

It is a sobering and frightening thought that there are "many" people who *think* that they know Christ and that their sins are forgiven, yet they do not know Him and they remain in their sin only to pay the price for eternity. For understanding's sake you could say that it is not a small number of people who falsely profess faith in Christ; no it is a very large number of people. How wonderful would it be to help inform a person of what true saving faith is according to the Bible and that person turn to Christ with saving faith?

The person who finally realizes that they do not really know Christ, though they have professed to, will then be able to truly seek the Savior and be forgiven. When they finally place their faith in Christ, they are forgiven and will inherit the kingdom of Heaven. Such a person would no longer be considered by Christ "a worker of lawlessness" (Matthew 7:23), but instead a son or daughter of righteousness. They can then rejoice with David saying, "¹Blessed is the one whose transgression is forgiven, whose sins are covered. ²Blessed is the man against whom the LORD counts no iniquity, and in whose spirit there is no deceit" (Psalm 32:1-2).

I'll give you a personal example of one such person who thought they were a Christian, and acted like one for 40 years, but after hearing a sermon series I preached on *Biblical faith*, this woman actually became a true follower of Christ. I had the opportunity to preach a set of services at a church in Texas one time, and I set out to preach on the Book of 1 John, which is written for the purpose of *knowing for sure that you know Christ* (1 John 5:13). In this series I preached on the characteristics of true faith and I gave the tests of true faith from 1 John. There was no one who walked forward to profess faith in Christ, but after I left that church and went home I received an email from one of the church members there. I was told that there was an older woman there that Sunday who had been a Sunday School teacher for 40 years and she actually walked forward that night after we left. She said that after hearing what the Bible actually said true saving faith is, that she had never really surrendered her life to Christ. That night she did.

Isn't that shocking that a person could be a Sunday School teacher for 40 years and a faithful church member, and yet not know Christ? This woman was one of a great number of people in churches today that had false assurance of their salvation, but thank the Lord that this woman heard the truth of God's Word and truly believed in Christ.

(5) The Bible commands us to examine ourselves to ensure that we know Christ.

The final reason to examine your faith, and certainly not the least important reason, is that the Bible commands you to. The Apostle Paul writes in 2 Corinthians 13:5, "⁵Examine yourselves, to see whether you are in the faith. Test yourselves. Or do you not realize this about yourselves, that Jesus Christ is in you?—unless indeed you fail to meet the test!" Every person in the church is charged with the responsibility of examining himself or herself.

Not only are we commanded to do this, but it is important to understand the wisdom of such a command. Think about this: if there are no second chances after death, and eternity is really as long as eternity is, and Hell is as bad as Hell is, then it would be wise to make sure that you know that you know Christ in the saving way.

The Apostle Peter wrote, "¹⁰Therefore, brothers, be all the more diligent to confirm your calling and election, for if you practice these qualities you will never fall" (2 Peter 1:10). We should be "diligent" or hardworking to make sure of our salvation.

Paul again writes to this effect in Philippians 2:12,

"¹²Therefore, my beloved, as you have always obeyed, so now, not only in my presence but much more in my absence, work out your own salvation with fear and trembling."

That is the purpose of these next chapters in this book. This book is designed with every "Christian" in mind. This is a tool that you can use to be "diligent" in confirming your salvation and to "examine yourselves, to see whether you are in the faith." In this book, we will examine what the Bible says real, authentic, saving faith is. It is my hope that as you read these pages you will either be shown that your faith is authentic and unto salvation or you will be shown that you have been falsely claiming to be a Christian. If so, my prayer is that you, after knowing what the Bible says you need to do, will choose then to truly, genuinely, and Biblically believe in Christ for the forgiveness of your sins and you will receive the promise of eternal life.

CHAPTER 2

Saving Faith is Living Faith

W E HAVE ALREADY looked at how the Bible teaches us that only the "righteous" will inherit eternal life (Matthew 25:46). We know that it is only the one who has faith in God who is considered righteous, and therefore it is absolutely necessary that we understand what *kind* of faith is genuine and authentic. That's what we'll be doing in the following chapters, is examining what the Bible says saving faith looks like.

Saving faith is lived out

According to Scripture, which is the Word of God, saving faith is a *living faith*. Said another way: saving faith is a faith that is lived out Habakkuk 2:4 says, "⁴the righteous shall live by his faith." The one who is made righteous before God by faith *lives* that faith out. Paul reemphasizes this and makes clear the true nature of saving faith is. In Romans 1:16-17 he writes, "¹⁶For I am not ashamed of the Gospel, for it is the power of God for salvation to everyone who believes, to the Jew first and also to the Greek. [17]For in it the righteousness of God is revealed from faith for faith, as it is written, "The righteous shall live by faith." Of course we know that the righteous are *made alive* by faith, which is a point in view here, but it is also true (as you can see from Romans 6-8) that the those who are made righteous by faith also *live* that same faith.

Authentic faith is not static. It is not without result. Saving faith is not a one-time faith that is expressed by a "profession of faith" made in a church service. Many people are under the false impression that *because* they made a profession of faith that they are saved. The Bible does not say that. The Bible says that, "the righteous shall live by faith." The person who has truly been justified by faith will live out that faith. There is so much more to being a Christian than simply naming the name of Christ at particular time or in a particular setting. No, authentic faith is the kind that is *lived out*.

Saving faith always leads to action

Faith is belief, and we know that if we believe something we will act on that belief, or we will operate under that belief. For instance, I can say that I believe in a chair, that it will support my weight, but until I actually have the conviction to sit in that chair, my belief falls short.

Hebrews 1:1-2 says this about the nature of Biblical faith, "[1]Now faith is the assurance of things hoped for, the conviction of things not seen. [2]For by it the people of old received their commendation." The Biblical idea of faith is assurance and conviction—which always leads to action, and you can tell this from the rest of the eleventh chapter of Hebrews.

Hebrews 11 demonstrates a formula of faith that goes like this: "By faith <u>this or that person</u> ***did*** this." Look at vs.8, "[8]By faith. Abraham obeyed when he was called to go out to a place that he was to receive as an inheritance. And he went out, not knowing where he was going." Genesis 12 gives us the account of Abraham's faith. Verse 1 says, "¹Now the LORD said to Abram, Go from your country and your kindred and your father's house to the land that I will show you." Verse 4 follows saying, "⁴So Abram went, as the LORD had told him, and Lot went with him. Abram was seventy-five years old when he departed from Haran." God spoke to Abraham and told him to leave, but He didn't tell him where he would be going, he said He would show him. The Lord was commanding Abraham to trust Him, and we know that Abraham believed God and went. If Abraham had not believed God, he would have remained in Haran. Abraham's "faith" would not have truly been faith without the action that followed. This is the kind of faith that is unto salvation. This is authentic faith. Genesis 15:6 says of Abraham, "⁶And he believed the LORD, and He counted it to him as righteousness." Abraham's faith was verified as true by his actions.

Now, I am not arguing that a person is saved by their works, because the Bible makes it clear that a person is not justified by the their good deeds. Good deeds do not erase bad deeds. Good works to not make up for sin. God forgives sin by His grace alone shown to those who believe in Him. What I am arguing is that the Bible clearly teaches that saving faith is proven by action; that when you believe in God you will act on that belief. A person is saved by faith, but only the *kind* of faith that is *living*.

Just like sitting in that chair proves that I believe in the properties of the chair, the actions of a person prove whether or not they are truly saved. This is the exact point of James 2. James writes, "¹⁴What good is it, my brothers, if someone says he has faith but does not have works? Can that faith save him? ¹⁵If a brother or sister is poorly clothed and lacking in daily food, ¹⁶and one of you says to them, "Go in peace, be warmed and filled," without giving them the things needed for the body, what good is that? ¹⁷So also faith by itself, if it does not have works, is dead" (James 2:14-16).

Faith that does not lead to action is not valid and it is not useful. A familiar saying is, "Put your money where your mouth is." When a person says that, they mean this: "if you really have faith that your team will win then put your money on the line." If you really believe in God, you really believe in Christ, then put yourself on the line. Live your belief. If you don't live it, you don't really believe it. And if you don't have that kind of faith, you don't have saving faith at all.

If you truly believe in Jesus Christ, you believe that He is God and that He is your Creator. Because He is your Creator, you are accountable to Him for your life and actions. If you truly believe that, then you will strive to make your actions pleasing to Him. It's not that you just believe mentally that there is a *possibility* that there is a God and that He will judge you; its that you *know* or are *convinced* that God exists and that He will judge you. Therefore, you live your life in relation to these truths. That is true faith, and that is the only kind that will please God as Hebrews 11:6 says, "⁶And without faith it is impossible to please Him, for whoever would draw near to God must believe that He exists and that He rewards those who seek Him."

Belief without action is not belief

Belief without action is really only *thought*, its acknowledgment that something *could be true*, but it's not good for anything. But here's a truth that is really eye-opening: Correct belief without action is useless. Good theology does not save a person. Take what James says, "[19]You believe that God is one; you do well. Even the demons believe—and shudder! [20]Do you want to be shown, you foolish person that faith apart from works is useless?" You see, the demons believe in God, and they believe all the correct things about God. They know that there will be judgment for sin, and they know Jesus Christ—in fact, they have seen Him and spoken with Him. However, the demons belief was not followed by obedience. They believe all the right things about God despite that fact, they went into rebellion against God. Their belief does not justify them before God in any way; rather, their belief and all their knowledge of Him only serve to condemn them even more. They *should* serve God. They *should* give Him the praise He is due. They *should* live for Him, but they refuse to. Their knowledge of God only makes their rebellion *worse*.

Knowing about God does not make you a Christian. Knowing the Bible does not make you a follower of Jesus. Being able to spout out correct theology does not make you a disciple of Jesus. Only the kind of faith that leads you to live for Christ is the kind of faith that saves you. James also points to Abraham to illustrate this: "[21]Was not Abraham our father justified by his works; [23]and the Scripture was fulfilled that says, "Abraham believed God, and it was counted to him as righteousness"—and he was called a friend of God. [24]You see that a person is justified by works and not by faith alone." Abraham's faith was authentic and proven by his deeds. But faith without works is false and useless. James 2:26 says, "[26]For as the body apart from the spirit is dead, so also faith apart from works is dead."

Authentic faith is not simply for Sundays

It is interesting that the Sunday nearest to Christmas and the Sunday of Mother's Day are the two most highly attended church services of the year in almost every church in America. If you were to take a poll of all the people who come to church on those two days, I believe that nearly everyone that comes would say that they are Christians and that they have been saved. I see so many new faces on those two Sundays, and those people don't come from out of town—they're local. When I introduce myself as the pastor to these new people, I usually receive the statement, "I know, I go to church here." They don't go to church here, in fact, they only come to church on those two Sundays. It is highly likely that they are not truly Christians because if they're not regularly a part of the Body of Christ, it is highly likely that they aren't living what they believe.

The same is true for so many people who attend churches every Sunday, but when they leave the church service they seem to leave Christ behind too. But, saving faith is not a faith that is only expressed on Sundays; it is a faith for every day.

When you read the words of the Apostle Paul as he describes the Christian's attitude going through life, you can sense the passion of the believer to live life for God. There is great passion to live in light of the fact that Jesus is Lord and that our lives are meant to be lived to please Him. Paul writes in 2 Corinthians 5:6-9, "⁶So we are always of good courage. We know that while we are at home in the body we are away from the Lord, ⁷for we walk by faith, not by sight. ⁸Yes, we are of good courage, and we would rather be away from the body and at home with the Lord. ⁹So whether we are at home or away, we make it our aim to please Him."

Now read vs.10, because it tells you what the believer

believes about God that makes him live the way he does. It is his *faith* that God is his judge. Verse 10 says, "¹⁰For we must all appear before the judgment seat of Christ, so that each one may receive what is due for what he has done in the body, whether good or evil." Scripture makes it clear that true faith is what drives the believer to *live* his faith. "And without faith it is impossible to please Him, for whoever would draw near to God must believe that He exists and that He rewards those who seek Him."

Listen to God's words to His people Israel concerning the *kind* of faith that they should approach Him with: "¹²Then you will call upon Me and come and pray to Me, and I will hear you. ¹³You will seek Me and find Me, when you seek Me with all your heart" (Jeremiah 29:12-13). Recall the account of Jesus' calling of the first disciples in the fifth chapter of the Gospel of Luke. Jesus went out on a boat with Peter, James, and John, and He told them to cast their nets out even though they had fished all night and had not caught anything. They trusted Jesus and obeyed. When they pulled the nets up the catch was so great that it took two boats and they were both sinking. Peter immediately fell at Jesus' feet, calling Him Lord. Jesus told Peter that He would make them fishers of men. Then you read verse 11, which says, "¹¹And when they had brought their boats to land, they left everything and followed Him." Because they believed in Jesus they left everything—all the fish, their nets, boats, family. They gave themselves completely over to following Jesus. The committed their lives to follow Him.

Saving faith is a sold-out, all-out, faith.

Just like the disciples abandoned everything to follow Jesus, so also is the attitude of all true followers of Christ.

Listen to the words of the Apostle Paul in Philippians 1:20-21, "²⁰It is my eager expectation and hope that I will not at all be ashamed, but that with full courage now as always Christ will be honored in my body, whether by life or by death. ²¹For to me to live is Christ, and to die is gain." Notice that Paul's faith is expressed in such a way that he can say that either in life or death that his aim is Christ. Read Galatians 2:20 also, "²⁰I have been crucified with Christ. It is no longer I who live, but Christ who lives in me. And the life I now live in the flesh I live by faith in the Son of God, who loved me and gave Himself for me."

Doing the Word of God evidences saving faith.

So how does a person *live* out their faith? How does a person *live* for Christ? A person lives like Christ by obeying His commands. Just like an apprentice follows his master, watches, learns, obeys, and imitates him, so also we are to watch, learn, obey, and imitate Christ. Obeying the Word of God shows saving faith, it shows that you really do follow Jesus and live in the reality that He is your Lord. Read Luke 8:19-21, "¹⁹Then His mother and His brothers came to Him, but they could not reach Him because of the crowd. ²⁰And He was told, "Your mother and Your brothers are standing outside, desiring to see You." ²¹But He answered them, "My mother and My brothers are those who hear the word of God and do it." Jesus only considers those who *obey* as those who are justified by faith. That is why He calls those who obey His relatives. True faith is obedient faith—it is lived out.

Look again at Jesus' words in Luke 11:27-28, "²⁷As He said these things, a woman in the crowd raised her voice and said to Him, "Blessed is the womb that bore You, and the breasts at which You nursed!" [28]But He said, "Blessed rather are those who hear the word of God and keep it." What an amazing reply! Jesus says that it is not those who are physically near Him who are blessed. No, it is only the ones who *keep* the word of God. Think about it in the most plain sense: if you believe God's Word, you will keep it; if you don't believe God's word, you won't keep it. Therefore, true, saving faith is living and evidenced by obedience.

When our lives have become marked by obedience to God, we can begin to have confidence that we know Him in the saving way. Read 1 John 2:3, "[3]And by this we know that we have come to know Him, if we keep His commandments." This is true belief: striving to live a life of obedience. This is what the heroes of faith are commended for in Hebrews 11. Person after person is mentioned in that chapter and all of them are mentioned for the same reason: they believed God and lived it out; they kept His commands. Look at what is said about Noah in Hebrews 11:7, "[7]By faith Noah, being warned by God concerning events yet unseen, in reverent fear constructed an ark for the saving of his household. By this he condemned the world and became an heir of the righteousness that comes by faith." We could go on and on with example after example of people in the Bible, who though they were imperfect, they *lived by faith.* By that living faith, they were justified and counted as righteous in God's sight.

If your faith is not living faith, it is not authentic, saving faith. You will live out what you believe.

CHAPTER 3

Saving Faith is Repentant Faith

WE HAVE SEEN in the previous chapter that saving faith is living faith. It is the kind of faith that leads to action, and the first action that follows saving faith is repentance. Repentance addresses the problem that all human beings have. The problem is that we are all guilty of living contrary to the way God created us to and we are guilty of breaking His laws.

God has authority over us because He created us.

We are all *creatures*, and it follows that creatures have *been created* by the Creator. Creatures are subject to the rule and authority of their Creator. Just as the potter has authority over the pot that he makes, so also God has authority over all of His creation. Jesus was able to calm the storms because He has authority over the winds and seas (Mark 4:35-41). Jesus was able to walk on water because He, as God, has power over the water (Matthew 14:22-27). Jesus was able to heal all manner of disease because He is sovereign over the human body and disease (Luke 4:40). These examples are just a small example of the authority that Jesus demonstrated over creation.

Because God has created us, He also has the right and authority to govern our living through His moral commandments. We know that He does this in love because God is love (1 John 4:8). However, when we break the law of God we are guilty of rebelling against His authority and design for Creation. This is what is called sin. Sin is *living for oneself* and not for God, obeying your own way and not the way of God. That is what Paul tells us in 2 Corinthians 5:15, that Christ died for us "that those who live might no longer live for themselves but for Him who for their sake died and was raised."

Sin is living as if God didn't exist.

Sin is rebellion against God. It's rebellion against God's law, and thereby living as an enemy of God. Sin is living and acting as if God didn't exist and didn't matter. Many people would not consider themselves atheists, but we are all guilty of *living* as atheists, that is, living as if we believed God didn't exist. At the least, sin is living practically as an atheist.

David describes human beings like this: "¹The fool says in his heart, "There is no God." They are corrupt, doing abominable iniquity; there is none who does good. ²God looks down from heaven on the children of man to see if there are any who understand, who seek after God. ³They have all fallen away; together they have become corrupt; there is none who does good, not even one" (Psalm 53:1-3). This is the kind of *practical atheism* that I am talking about. When man does whatever he wants, however he wants, whenever he wants, without regard for God's commands, he is living as a *practical atheist*.

The Apostle Paul writes about man going his own way and doing his own thing without regard for God's commands. He states, "¹⁰None is righteous, no, not one; ¹¹no one understands; no one seeks for God. ¹²All have turned aside together they have become worthless; no one does good, not even one" (Romans 3:10-12). The prophet Isaiah tells that Christ had to die for us to pay the penalty for our sin, which is our rebellion against God, our turning from God's way. Isaiah writes, "⁶All we like sheep have gone astray; we have turned—every one—to his own way; and the LORD has laid on Him the iniquity of us all."

If you recall the sin of Adam and Eve you can see very clearly that they sinned by turning from God's command and obeying themselves. In Genesis 3 we read of how Adam and Eve were tempted and then we are told *why* they sinned. Genesis 3:6 says, "⁶So when the woman saw that the tree was good for food, and that it was a delight to the eyes, and that the tree was to be desired to make one wise, she took of its fruit and ate, and she also gave some to her husband who was with her, and he ate." The first man and woman were longing to please themselves rather than God and they broke His command to do it. The Apostle John explains to us that the nature of all sin is the selfish pleasing of the body in a way that is contrary to God's commands. He writes in 1 John 2:16, "¹⁶For all that is in the world—the desires of the flesh and the desires of the eyes and the pride of life—is not from the Father but is from the world."

This pattern of temptation is also at the core of the temptations that Christ faced in the wilderness (Luke 4:1-13). Jesus was tempted with the *lust of the* flesh (tempted to turn stone into bread); the lust of the eyes (to inherit the kingdoms of the world); and the boastful pride of life (to test God by jumping off the pinnacle of the temple). Christ overcame these temptations through the power of the Holy Spirit (Luke 4:1) and the power of the Word of God (vs.4, 8, 12).

Worshiping and Serving the Creature rather than the Creator

Adam and Eve were guilty of worshipping and serving themselves, the creatures, rather than the Creator. That's what we all do when we sin; we worship and serve our own selfish desires at the expense of disobeying God. Its not that God does not want what is best for us, but God does want the best for us and that's why He's given us His commands. When we follow our own way only death and destruction follow. The Apostle Paul says that just like Adam and Eve, we are all guilty of worshipping our own sinful desires rather than God. He writes that we "exchanged the truth about God for a lie and worshipped and served the creature rather than the Creator who is blessed forever! Amen" (Romans 1:25). He also says it like this: "²¹For although they knew God, they did not honor Him as God or give thanks o Him, but they became futile in their thinking, and their foolish hearts were darkened. ²²Claiming to be wise, they became fools, ²³and exchanged the glory of the immortal God for images resembling mortal man and birds and animals and creeping things" (Romans 1:21-23).

What is repentance?

Sin is self-governing idolatry, and that is exactly what God calls us to turn away from. He has called us to change our ways from worshipping and serving the creature rather than the Creator. That's what repentance is. Repentance means that you turn from one course of action and go the opposite way. It is essentially doing a U-turn in life. We have all lived for ourselves and lived our own way and God calls us to stop, turn around, and begin to live our lives for Him. This is the reason Christ died for us! Look at what the Apostle Peter writes in 1 Peter 2:24, "²⁴He Himself bore our sins in His body on the tree, that we might die to sin and live to righteousness. By His wounds you have been healed."

Saving faith is always proven by repentance, and repentance of sin is an essential act of true faith. Paul writes, "¹⁴For the love of Christ controls us, because we have concluded this: that one died for all, therefore all have died; ¹⁵and He died for all, that those who live might no longer live for themselves but for Him who for their sake died and was raised." As you can see, if you are truly a believer in Jesus and have truly surrendered your life to Him as your Savior and Lord, it follows that you will indeed turn from serving yourself (your old master) and turn to serve Jesus (your new Master).

Repentance is a matter of allegiance.

I am an American, and when I say the Pledge of Allegiance I am vowing that it is my duty not only to honor my country and her Constitution, but that I recognize that if I am called upon, I will lay down my life for her freedom. My pledge of allegiance is one of life and death. So also is the surrendering of your life to Christ. Whereas you were living and dying for yourself, now you have pledged your allegiance to Christ, to both live and die for Him. This is what the Thessalonian Church was commended for by the Apostle Paul, "⁹For they themselves report concerning us the kind of reception we had among you, and how you turned to God from idols to serve the living and true God…" (1 Thessalonians 1:9).

We know that John the Baptist preached repentance as the means to prepare for the Messiah to come into the world saying "Repent, for the kingdom of heaven is at hand" (Matthew 3:2). John was preparing the world for the arrival of her King, her Creator, and repentance was the way to do it. It may be helpful to think of it like this: if a king were coming to your country to rule over it you would either count your troops and evaluate your armory to determine if you could withstand him, or you would send out a flag of surrender and submit to serve the new king. That is exactly what John the Baptist was calling people to do, and that is exactly what we are called to do. We are invited to serve Jesus and be forgiven of our sins, or else we will be judged for our sins and be found guilty.

Read this amazing passage where the Apostle Paul describes his own attitude of repentance and allegiance to Christ: "[20]I have been crucified with Christ. It is no longer I who live, but Christ who lives in me. And the life I now live in the flesh I live by faith in the Son of God, who loved me and gave Himself for me" (Galatians 2:20). Paul had surrendered his entire self to Christ so that he could say, "[20]It is my eager expectation and hope that I will not be at all ashamed, but that with full courage now as always Christ will be honored in my body, whether by life or by death. [21]For to me to live is Christ, and to die is gain."

Repentance is an essential part of salvation.

Repentance is a key and essential part of saving faith. Think of it this way, when you truly believe that God is your Creator and that you are accountable to Him, you will strive to change your course of action from self-serving to submissive service to God. That is what was commanded time and time again in Scripture, that all people repent of their sin and prepare to meet God. That is the message that John the Baptist was sent to preach to prepare people to meet Jesus: "¹In those days John the Baptist came preaching in the wilderness of Judea, ²"Repent, for the kingdom of heaven is at hand."

Repentance of sin is the message that Jesus preached throughout His ministry as well: "¹⁷From that time Jesus began to preach, saying, "Repent, for the kingdom of heaven is at hand." If that is the message that Jesus Himself preached and yet you do not repent of your sin, can you actually say you believe Him? I think not. No, either you do not believe Jesus or you do and you are simply rebelling against the command He's given you to turn from your sinning and follow Him.

Not only was repentance the message of John the Baptist and Jesus, it was also the message of the Apostles. Acts 2:38 says, "³⁸And Peter said to them, "Repent and be baptized every one of you in the name of Jesus Christ for the forgiveness of your sins, and you will receive the gif of the Holy Spirit." Peter also preached in Acts 3:19, "¹⁹Repent therefore, and turn back, that your sins may be blotted out." The Apostle Paul preached in Acts 17:30, "³⁰The times of ignorance God overlooked, but now He commands all people everywhere to repent."

Repentance is such an essential part of saving faith that the Apostle John declares that a person that does not repent of their sin does not know God. He writes, "⁶No one who abides in Him keeps on sinning; non one who keeps sinning has either seen Him or known Him. ⁷Little children, let no one deceive you. Whoever practices righteousness is righteous, as He is righteous" (1 John 3:6-7). He also writes in 1 John

3:10, "¹⁰By this it is evident who are the children of God, and who are the children of the devil: whoever does not practice righteousness is not of God, nor is the one who does not love his brother." Notice that he says, "by this it is *evident* who are the children of God" [emphasis mine]. What is it that makes the children of God evident? The practicing of righteousness, not the practicing of unrighteousness makes them known. Why, because the children of God are those who have believed in Christ and repented of their sin. You can tell they love God because they have forsaken their sin and are now in pursuit of Him and obedience to His commands. "³For this is the love of God, that we keep His commandments. And His commandments are not burdensome" (1 John 5:3).

Saving faith is proven immediately by repentance.

When a person truly believes in Jesus, they will immediately being repenting of sin. Yes, repentance is something that takes time and is a process, but it is also something that happens immediately. Remember that repentance is a change of heart, a change of allegiance, and a change of the course of action of your life.

Look at the man in Scripture named Zacchaeus in Luke 19:5-10, "⁵And when Jesus came to the place, He looked up and said to him, "Zacchaeus, hurry and come down, for I must stay at your house today." ⁶So he hurried and came down and received Him joyfully. ⁷And when they saw it, they all grumbled, "He has gone in to be the guest of a man who is a sinner." ⁸And Zacchaeus stood and said to the Lord, "Behold, Lord, the half of my goods I give to the poor. And if I have defrauded anyone of anything, I restore it fourfold." ⁹And Jesus said to him, "Today salvation has come to this house, since he also is a son of Abraham. [10]For the Son of Man came to seek and to save the lost." Zacchaeus immediately began repenting of his fraudulent actions. He had stolen from people and abused his authority as a tax collector to oppress others. But upon believing in Jesus he immediately began the opposite course of action.

Remember also the testimony of the Apostle Paul, who was on his way to Damascus to persecute Christians and gather them up, but on the road he was encountered by the risen Lord Jesus Christ (Acts 9). After being called by Christ to follow Him, Paul changed his course of action immediately and became a preacher of Christ rather than a persecutor of Christ.

The call to repentance is an invitation of grace.

There is a startling encounter in Luke 13:1-3 between Jesus and a group of people who were affected by tragedy. In this encounter Jesus tells us that the most important thing that a person could ever do it to repent of their sin and turn to God in faith. Without faith and repentance a person is condemned to hell for eternity and there is no suffering comparable to that. Read Jesus' words in Luke 13:1-3, "[1]There were some present at that very time who told Him about the Galileans whose blood Pilate had mingled with their sacrifices. [2]And He answered them, "Do you think that these Galileans were worse sinners than all the other Galileans, because they suffered in this way? [3]No, I tell you; but unless you repent, you will all likewise perish. [4]Or those eighteen on whom the tower of Siloam fell and killed them: do you think that they were worse offenders than all the others who lived in Jerusalem? [5]No, I tell you; but unless you repent, you will all likewise perish."

God is not obligated to give us opportunity to repent, but Jesus graciously preached repentance to all. If God were to give us justice for our sin (rebellion) against Him, we would all spend eternity in hell. But God graciously gives us all the opportunity to repent of our sin and He invites us to follow Him. In fact, the time that we have on this earth is meant to be our opportunity to be made right with Him through faith and repentance. Look at Romans 2:3-4, "³Do you suppose, O man—you who judge those who practice such things and yet do them yourself—that you will escape the judgment of God? ⁴Or do you presume on the riches of His kindness and forbearance and patience, not knowing that God's kindness is meant to lead you to repentance?"

God is not obligated to give you opportunity to repent, but He does because He is gracious. He is looking for people to repent and He joyously receives all who come to Him in faith in repentance. Remember that Jesus said, "there is joy before the angels of God over one sinner who repents" (Luke 15:10).

The ability to repent is a gift of grace.

The Bible makes it clear that God is the one who grants repentance. He does this in at least two ways. First, God grants repentance by giving a person the opportunity or time to repent. He doesn't immediately end the lives of sinners and judge them for their sin. No, if you have had life you have had opportunity to get right with God, and the life you have in you now is time and opportunity. Secondly, God grants repentance to a person by changing their heart and granting them new desires. This is what is called the "new birth" (John 3). This is a supernatural miracle that God performs by grace in the heart of every person who truly believes in

Him. When He does this, He makes the person new and gives them a new heart and new desires that are holy and righteous (2 Corinthians 5:17). God delivers them from their bondage to sin and frees them to follow Him (John 8:36).

Look at 2 Timothy 2:24-26 as Paul writes to young Timothy to teach him that he needs to be careful how he deals with those who oppose him because God may be gracious to them and grant them repentance. Paul writes, "[24]And the Lord's servant must not be quarrelsome but kind to everyone, able to teach, patiently enduring evil, [25]correcting his opponents with gentleness. God may perhaps grant them repentance leading to a knowledge of the truth, [26]and they may come to their senses and escape from the snare of the devil, after being captured by him to do his will" (2 Timothy 2:24-26). Also look at the reaction of this group in the Book of Acts: "When they heard these things they fell silent. And they glorified God, saying, "Then to the Gentiles also God has granted repentance that leads to life" (Acts 11:18).

Repentance is an act of saving faith.

We have looks at this in quite a bit of detail, that saving faith and repentance is inseparable. In fact, repentance is the first action of saving faith. It is the forsaking of disobedience towards God and the embracing of Him as your Lord and Savior. Whereas you once lived without regard for God and as His enemy through rebellion, you now seek to live for Him and follow Him. This is why Jesus says, "[15]If you love Me, you will keep My commandments" (John 14:15) and "[24]Whoever does not love Me does not keep My words. And the word that you hear is not Mine but the Fathers' who sent Me." If we love God, we will obey Him. If we truly believe in Him we will strive to live for Him. Just as John said, "³For this is the love of God, that we keep His commandments" (1 John 5:3).

If your life is not marked by repentance of sin, it is very likely that you do not know God. If you refuse to repent of your sin, you can be guaranteed that you do not know God because, "⁶No one who abides in Him keeps on sinning; no one who keeps sinning has either seen Him or known Him" (1 John 3:6).

Saving faith is repentant faith, and God is waiting with arms wide open for the one who comes to Him in faith and repentance (see the whole chapter of Luke 15). "Just so, I tell you, there is joy before the angels of God over one sinner who repents" (Luke 15:10).

CHAPTER 4

The Fruit of Saving Faith

I HAVE POINTED out earlier that saving faith always leads to action. That action can be properly characterized as fruit. Just as you can know a tree by the fruit it produces, so also you can know if a person is really a true disciple of Christ by the "fruit" of their life. In fact, Jesus Himself teaches us that we can know who the false teachers in this world are by examining the fruit of their lives. Jesus said in Matthew 7:15-16, "15Beware of false prophets, who come to you in sheep's clothing but inwardly are ravenous wolves. 16You will recognize them by their fruits. Are grapes gathered from thorn bushes, or figs from thistles?" You can know if you personally are a true follower of Christ if you examine the fruit of your life.

We know that saving faith produces fruit. In Luke 8 Jesus teaches a parable on different kinds of soils. His metaphor is such that the soils represent the different types of hearers of the Gospel, and the seed that is cast out on them is the Gospel message. The "hard path" soil receives seed, but is too hardened to receive it. So the birds come and eat the seed and the rest is trampled under foot. So it is with the hard-hearted man who cannot receive the Gospel. The second type of soil is rocky. This soil receives the seed and a plant springs up quickly, but because the soil is shallow the plant doesn't grow deep roots. Soon, the plant dies because of lack of depth and moisture. So it is with the person who receives the Gospel in a very shallow sense, but when testing times come they fall away because they lack roots and depth. The third type of soil is filled with thorns. It receives the seed and the plant grows but is soon choked out by the thorns. So it is with the one who receives the Gospel but it is soon choked out by the cares of the world. The fourth soil is good. It receives the seed, grows the plant, and produces much fruit. This last instance is the only one of the four that is pleasing God. The one that endures and produces fruit is the one that truly believes and inherits eternal life.

Those who truly believe will produce fruit because upon faith, God makes that person a new creation. This is a supernatural act of God whereby He transforms a person's heart and makes them completely new. This is exactly what Jesus was teaching Nicodemus in John 3:5-7, "⁵Jesus answered, "Truly, truly, I say to you, unless one is born of water and the Spirit, he cannot enter the kingdom of God. ⁶That which is born of the flesh is flesh, and that which is born of the Spirit is spirit. ⁷Do not marvel that I said to you, 'You must be born again.'" God promises us that when we come to Christ in faith that He will indeed make us "born again." Paul teaches us in 2 Corinthians 5:17 that, "¹⁷Therefore, if anyone is in Christ, he is a new creation. The old has passed away; behold, the new has come."

How does God make me new?

Before Christ forgives you and God makes you a new creation, you are in bondage to sin and enslaved to the sinful desires of the body. Romans 8:7-8 says, "⁷For the mind that is set on the flesh is hostile to God, for it does not submit to God's law; indeed it cannot. ⁸Those who are in the flesh cannot please God." That is the tragic state that we find ourselves in without Christ. Without His freeing power we are in bondage to our sin, unable to please God. But the first fruit that God brings forth in a believer's life is that He gives you a new heart and places His Holy Spirit within you." Continuing in Romans 8 and looking at verse 9, Paul writes, "⁹You, however, are not in the flesh but in the Spirit, if in fact the Spirit of God dwells in you. Anyone who does not have the Spirit of Christ does not belong to Him." When Christ saves us we are no longer enslaved to the sin, but now we are able to serve God because He has placed His Spirit within us.

God gives believers a new heart with all its new desires and joys. This is the promise of God that He made to us long ago. God said in Ezekiel 36:25-27, "²⁵I will sprinkle clean water on you, and you shall be clean from all your uncleanness, and from all your idols I will cleanse you. ²⁶And I will give you a new heart, and a new spirit I will put within you. And I will remove the heart of stone from your flesh and give you a heart of flesh. ²⁷And I will put My Spirit within you, and cause you to walk in all My statutes and be careful to obey My rules." What a marvelous promise to all who believe in Christ!

The fact that God does this within every single believer is the reason why I contend that true saving faith *always* produces the proof of fruit.

Why is it important to examine the fruit of my life?

We have looked extensively at Jesus' frightening words concerning the Day of Judgment and how many people will be turned away from Heaven even though they were fully convinced that they knew Jesus. Jesus said in Luke 7:21, "²¹Not everyone who says to Me, 'Lord, Lord,' will enter the kingdom of heaven, but the one who does the will of My Father who is in heaven. ²²On that day many will say to Me, 'Lord, Lord, did we not prophesy in Your name, and cast out demons in Your name, and do many mighty works in Your name? ²³And then will I declare to them, 'I never knew you; depart from Me, you workers of lawlessness.'" If only those people had examined the fruit of their lives they would have known that they didn't know Jesus. They would have been able to tell that they needed to be made right with God through the Savior. But on that day it will be too late to do anything about it.

You can tell the differences between if you are a true believer in Jesus or someone who is not. The Bible sometimes uses figurative language to talk about things. In Matthew 13:24-30, Jesus refers to His true believers as "wheat" and all others as "darnel" or "tares." Without a quick word on wheat farming this metaphor may seem a bit confusing.

The last couple of places that I have lived have been heavily dependent on farming. The major crops included peanuts, cotton, and wheat. Getting to know the people who live in these areas has really opened my eyes to the truth of Scripture and some particular teachings of Jesus are made very clear to me now. When Jesus talks about wheat and tares growing up in the same field it really is quite a vivid picture. You see, wheat and tares are almost identical in appearance, but completely different in substance. Wheat is good for food, as you harvest the heads and use them for all kinds of food products. Tares are not useful, in any way and in fact can be deadly.

Tares are known by the name of "darnel" or "false wheat." Our local famers call it "cheet." Darnel can cause so many problems for farmers. It carries a fungus on it that has been known to parasitize entire wheat fields. It is also toxic. If ingested, it makes you feel drunken and dizzy and can even cause death. In, the French word for tares is actually translated "intoxicated" and the Latin name means "drunk."

It is very important to know the difference between true and false wheat, and even more important to know the difference between true faith Christ and false professions. The way that you tell the difference in both is by examining the fruit. Wheat and tares are almost identical until the head of the plant appears. The wheat turns golden brown, while the tares turn black. While the wheat is good for food, the tare is deadly and utterly useless—as is falsely claiming Christ.

What is the fruit of saving faith?

If we can examine the fruit of our lives and know whether or not we know Christ in the saving way, then we need to know what fruit to look for. The first fruit that is evident with saving faith is repentance. Have you begun to repent of your sin (turn from sin and strive for righteousness)? Since that is part of the requirement for coming to Christ, that you repent, then you can know whether or not you truly believe by whether or not you begin repenting of sin. The true believer's life is marked by constant repentance. As you are made more like Jesus, you are repenting of sin and embracing His way of life for you. God is making His children like Jesus and we know this from Romans 8:29, "[29]For those whom He foreknew He also predestined to be conformed to the image of His son, in order that He might be the firstborn among many brothers." As God conforms you to be like Christ you will be shedding of your old ways and embracing His.

The Bible also tells us that God calls those who are His children to constantly repent by His Holy Spirit living inside them. James 4:5 says, "He yearns jealously over the Spirit that He has made to dwell within us." When God saves a person He actively works in their life to make them holy. He graciously frees us from sin and calls us to follow Him, and when we don't He is jealous over us and for us such that He will bring us back to Him.

As a person grows in Christ-likeness, the Bible tells us that there are certain fruits that the Holy Spirit grows in a person's life. Galatians 5:22-24 says, "[22]But the fruit of the Spirit is love, joy, peace, patience, kindness, goodness, faithfulness, [23]gentleness, self-control; against such things there is no law. [24]And those who belong to Christ Jesus have crucified the flesh with its passions and desires." If you are truly God's child, you should begin seeing yourself grow in these areas. It does not happen overnight. This growth is a process, as sometimes we experience great amounts of growth and other times it seems we are moving slowly. Regardless of the rate of growth, you should be becoming more loving, joyful, peaceful, patient, kind, good, faithful, gentle, and self-controlled.

Jesus tells us that true believes will indeed bear the fruit of love in their lives. He said, "[34]A new commandment I give to you, that you love one another: just as I have loved you, you also are to love one another. [35]By this all people will know that you are My disciples, if you have love for one another" (John 13:34-35). The Apostle John writes, "[14]We know that we have passed out of death and into life, because we love the brothers. Whoever does not love abides in death"(1 John 3:14). The people of God are marked by the fruit of love one for another. In fact, John goes on to state that, "²⁰If anyone says "I love God," and hates his brother, he is a liar; for he who does not love his brother whom he has seen cannot love God whom he has not seen"(1 John 4:20). If you are not able to love others when God has so graciously forgiven and loved you, then it is likely that you yourself have not experienced the grace, forgiveness, and love of God.

The Apostle Paul gives another list of fruits that should be growing and showing in a believer's life. He writes in Colossians 3:12-14, "¹²Put on then, as God's chosen ones, holy and beloved, compassionate hearts, kindness, humility, meekness, and patience, ¹³bearing with one another and, if one has a complaint against another, forgiving each other; as the Lord has forgiven you, so you also must forgive. ¹⁴And above all these put on love, which binds everything together in perfect harmony." These are characteristics that the members of God's Church are to be showing more and more. If you have not seen these fruits in your life or a growth in them then something is wrong.

Jesus tells us that the more we "abide" in Him, the more fruit that we will bear. in John 15:4-5 He says, "⁴Abide in Me, and I in you. As the branch cannot bear fruit by itself, unless it abides in the vine, neither can you, unless you abide in Me. ⁵I am the vine, you are the branches. Whoever abides in Me and I in him, he it is that bears much fruit, for apart from Me you can do nothing." If you are bearing fruit it is because God is working in you and you are abiding in Him—striving to live for Him and seeking after Him through His Word, preaching, teaching, and fellowship with His people. If you are not growing in these fruits, it is because you are not abiding in

Him, because you cannot do anything apart from Him. If you are not producing any of these fruits it is likely that you do not know Christ and are still dead in your sins. You must believe in Jesus and repent and follow after Him.

Jesus said in Mark 12:30-31 that the greatest commandment is that "You shall love the Lord your God with all your heart and with all your soul and with all your mind and with all your strength" and that the second greatest commandment is "you shall love your neighbor as yourself." If you are a true believer in Christ you should be growing in love for God and for others. Jesus even tells us in Matthew 25 that the difference in true believers and false believers are that true believers *lived* their love for God. They lived their love for God by helping and loving the hungry, the thirsty, the stranger, the naked, the sick, and the imprisoned.

Dying fruit

There are many fruits of the sinful ways of life that you should be fleeing as well. These fruits should not be growing, and their presence ought to be fading. Paul gives us a list of these sinful fruits that should be dying in Galatians 5:19-21, "[19]Now the works of the flesh are evidence: sexual immorality, impurity, sensuality, [20]idolatry, sorcery, enmity, strife, jealousy, fits of anger, rivalries, dissensions, divisions, [21]envy, drunkenness, orgies, and things like these. I warn you, as I warned you before, that those who do such things will not inherit the kingdom of God."

As the Spirit of God works in your life you should be putting those sins to death and walking more in more in righteousness. Paul tells us in Galatians 5 that it by the power of the Holy Spirit that we are going to walk more in righteousness and less in sin. He writes in Galatians 5:16, "¹⁶But I say, walk by the Spirit, and you will not gratify the desires of the flesh." If God has saved you, He will not stop there but will continue working in you through His Spirit, and it is His Spirit within you making you to walk in holiness. "¹⁰For we are His workmanship, created in Christ Jesus for good works, which God prepared beforehand, that we should walk in them" (Ephesians 2:10).

Examine yourself.

If you have not been seeing these changes taking place and these fruits being produced then it is my prayer that you examine and think very seriously about whether or not you have truly gone to Jesus for forgiveness with a repentant heart. The Lord forgives all those who truly believe and call on Him for forgiveness, "For everyone who calls on the name of the Lord will be saved" (Romans 10:13).

Will you take this time to examine your life? If you have found that you don't have a saving relationship with Jesus, then please make that right with Him. "⁹If you confess with your mouth that Jesus is Lord and believe in your heart that God raised Him from the dead, you will be saved. ¹⁰For with the heart one believes and is justified, and with the mouth one confesses and is saved. ¹¹For the Scripture says, "Everyone who believes in Him will not be put to shame" (Romans 10:9-11).

CHAPTER 5
Saving Faith Endures

WE HAVE LOOKED a number of times at the haunting words of Jesus in Matthew 7:21 when He said, "²¹Not everyone who says to Me, 'Lord, Lord,' will enter the kingdom of heaven, but the one who does the will of My Father who is in heaven." Undoubtedly, there are many in the world today who at one time "followed the Lord" but now are far from Him. It is likely that those people have been falsely assured that they know Jesus even though they don't follow Him and obey Him. Those people may have once professed faith in Christ, but they don't endure to the end. They could be best characterized by the type of person Jesus talked about in Luke 8 that hear the Gospel but "as they go on their way they are choked by the cares and riches and pleasures of life, and their fruit does not mature" (Luke 8:14). It is clear that this kind of person, one that never bears fruit spiritually, is really not a true believer in Christ. That kind of person does not possess saving faith.

Have you ever wondered why over a period of time it seems that so many people fall away from the Lord? It is a sad occasion when someone quits on Christ. Usually people refer to this sort of thing as "backsliding", which is the idea that a person is still "saved" or "born again" but that they are simply living in sin. Certainly, there are times when believers in Christ fall into sin, as we all know that we are sinners. In fact 1 John 1:8 says, "⁸If we say we have no sin, we deceive ourselves, and the truth is not in us." Let's have this understanding as we proceed in this chapter, because I want to make sure you understand that true believers in Christ are not perfect and sinless. On the contrary, we all have things we struggle with and will continue to struggle with until the day we die.

With that being said, it is a Biblical principle that the kind of faith that is saving is the kind of faith that endures to the end. In this chapter I'm going to give you nine Biblical proofs to show you that true saving faith endures to the end.

1) Saving faith is enduring because God makes you a new creation.

We saw in the last chapter that saving faith *always* produces fruit because that fruit is a result of God making a person a new creation. 2 Corinthians 5:17 says, "¹⁷Therefore, if anyone is in Christ, he is a new creation. The old has passed away; behold, the new has come." That means that when a person finally believes in Christ and comes to Him in repentance that God performs a supernatural work by making them a new person. This is what Jesus referred to as being "born again." Jesus taught Nicodemus that it is necessary for a person to be born again to enter heaven because heaven is not a place for those who haven't been transformed (John 3).

When a person is born again, that's the end of it. There is no teaching in all of Scripture of a person being "un-born again." There is no teaching in all of Scripture of a person being changed back into an old creation. So when a person is born again, that's what they are forever. This is why saving faith will always endure to the end.

2) *Eternal* life is the fundamental promise made to all those who believe in Christ.

Saving faith will always endure to the end because the promise of eternal life is given to all who call upon the name of the Lord for salvation (Joel 2:32, Acts 2:21, Romans 10:13). Eternal life is not something that begins upon death, but rather it begins upon saving faith. Just as I just pointed out that no one can be "un-born again", it is necessary to understand that when a person comes to Jesus through faith and repentance that He immediately regenerates them (makes them born again). Jesus said in John 5:24, "24Truly, truly, I say to you, whoever hears My word and believes Him who sent Me has eternal life. He does not come into judgment, but has passed from death to life."

Eternal life is something that immediately happens and eternally endures. This is why a person who has saving faith will endure in that faith through the end. A person is immediately and eternally made a new creation, made after the image of Christ, sealed with the Holy Spirit as a guarantee from God (Ephesians 1:13).

(3) Faith that endures to the end is proof that you are a true believer.

In Scripture, God makes it clear that the kind of faith that is saving is the kind that lasts. Paul said, "4as servants of God we commend ourselves in every way: by great endurance…" (2 Corinthians 6:4). The Apostle John gives us assurance that when a person abides in their faith in Christ that they are truly abiding in Christ. He writes, "²⁴Let what you heard from the beginning abide in you. If what you heard from the beginning abides in you, then you too will abide in the Son and in the Father." That's just the nature of saving faith—it stands the test of time and trials.

The writer of the Book of Hebrews gives warning to the members of the church when he writes, "¹²Take care, brothers, lest there be in any of you an evil, unbelieving heart, leading you to fall away from the living God. ¹³But exhort one another every day, as long as it is called "today," that none of you may be hardened by the deceitfulness of sin. ¹⁴For we have come to share in Christ, if indeed we hold our original confidence firm to the end." Notice that he didn't say that a person can "lose their salvation." What he wrote was that a person can know that they have "come to share in Christ" if they hold to their original confidence (their faith) to the end. The writer of Hebrews can say that because it is true. There are those who seemed to know Christ, and did many of the things that Christians do, but they never truly knew Christ and that is made apparent by the fact that they don't hold their faith to the end. Perseverance is an essential characteristic of saving faith.

4) Abandoning the faith means that you were never in the faith to begin with.

People that abandon the faith don't lose their salvation. The fact is that there was no salvation to be lost in them. Look at what the Apostle John writes about false teachers (false converts) in 1 John 2:19, "¹⁹They went out from us, but they were not of us; for if they had been of us, they would have continued with us. But they went out, that it might become plain that they all are not of us." Do you see what gave them away as false converts? It was the fact that they did not endure. They did not stand the test of time and trials.

It is not possible to "fall from grace." If a person seems to fall away from grace it is likely because they were never born again in the first place.

Now, it is possible for believers to fall into sin through spiritual neglect and temptation, but a true believer will always be brought back to faith and repentance because they have been made a new creation and because the Holy Spirit o God is living within them. The Bible tells us clearly that it is the Holy Spirit that draws us back into repentance as our sin grieves Him (Ephesians 4:30) and because God "He yearns jealously over the Spirit that He has made to dwell in us" (James 4:5). This is why a person who is truly saved will never truly fall away from the faith.

5) Since the work of Christ in salvation is complete, true believers endure to the end.

God makes it certain to us in His Word that the work that Christ does in salvation is complete. This point touches back on the first point that was made about a person being unable to be "un-born again." You see, when a person comes Christ in faith and repentance God forgives them completely and eternally. This is because the complete debt of sin was nailed to the cross of Christ—there is no more penalty to be paid for those who are in Christ. Colossians 2:13-14 says, "¹³And you, who were dead in your trespasses and the uncircumcision of your flesh, God made alive together with Him, having forgiven us all our trespasses, ¹⁴by canceling the record of debt that stood against us with its legal demands. This He set aside, nailing it to the cross." God makes a person "alive together with Him [Christ]" by forgiving us completely and making us new creatures.

The Apostle Paul tells us that this salvation that God grants to believers is not temporary state, but rather a permanent change of destination. He writes in Colossians 1:13-14, "¹³He has delivered us from the domain of darkness and transferred us to the kingdom of His beloved Son, ¹⁴in whom we have redemption, the forgiveness of sins." That's amazing! All of that happens to a believer when they come to Christ in faith and repentance.

Paul further makes the point clear that believers are completely "justified by His blood" and "saved by Him from the wrath of God", and He rejoices that those in Christ "have now received reconciliation" (Romans 5:9, 11). Justification, peace, and reconciliation have been given completely. They are not temporary gifts.

6) True believers endure to the end because God guards them.

God loves His children, and He protects them. That's why we can be assured that those who truly belong to Him will endure to the end. Listen to the words of Jesus, "²⁷My sheep hear My voice, and I know them, and they follow Me. ²⁸I give them eternal life, and they will never perish, and no one will snatch them out of My hand. ²⁹My Father, who has given them to Me, is greater than all, and no one is able to snatch them out of the Father's hand. ³⁰I and the Father are one" (John

10:27-29). Jesus and the Father guard His disciples all the way until they stand before Him and through eternity. This is why Jesus always brings a Christian who has gone astray back to Himself. He compares it to a shepherd who brings back a wandering sheep (Luke 15:3-7).

The Apostle Paul was rightfully convinced of God's power to keep him through all the trials and difficulties that he faced in his lifetime and ministry for Christ. He wrote in 2 Timothy 1:12, "¹²But I am not ashamed, for I know whom I have believed, and I am convinced that He is able to guard until that Day what has been entrusted to me." Paul was certain that he was safe in the arms of Christ because he knew that God is faithful to guard His own, just as the Apostle Peter wrote to believers by saying that they were given "⁴an inheritance that is imperishable, undefiled, and unfading, kept in heaven for you, ⁵who by God's power are being guarded through faith for a salvation ready to be revealed in the last time."

7) **True believers endure because God is faithful to continue His work in them.**

Because God does not abandon believers to themselves, but continues to work in their life, they will endure to the end. Paul wrote in Philippians 1:6, "⁶And I am sure of this, that He who began a good work in you will bring it to completion at the day of Jesus Christ." You see, true believers keep in the faith because God keeps them in the faith. God, who began working in the heart through faith and salvation, will continue to work in the heart unto completion. This is a guarantee.

A Paul wrote to the young believers in the Church at

Thessalonica, he reassured them that God would continue to keep them and work in their hearts to completion. He wrote to them, "²³Now may the God of peace Himself sanctify you completely, and may your whole spirit and soul and body be kept blameless at the coming of our Lord Jesus Christ. ²⁴He who calls you is faithful; He will surely do it." Notice how Paul places all of the work on God's strength. He says that it is God who sanctifies (makes one righteous and holy); it is God who keeps one blameless through Christ; it is God who calls you to salvation; it is God who continues faithfully to keep you. That is an amazing guarantee to all believers in Christ, and that is how we know that true believers will endure in their faith to the end.

8) True believers endure to the end because God is faithful to preserve them.

In 2 Timothy 2:13, Paul told Timothy that even "¹³if we are faithless, He remains faithful—for He cannot deny Himself." God keeps us believing in Him because He is eternally faithful to His promise to do so. We have the guarantee that even when we are struggling and don't have much strength, that God will never abandon us. It would be safe to say that if God did abandon us when we were struggling that none of us would be able to remain in the faith, but thanks be to God that He is faithful to keep us!

The Israelites celebrated the faithfulness of God for good reason. In the Psalms one can read over and over about the steadfast love of the Lord. Psalm 100:5 says, "⁵For the LORD is good; His steadfast love endures forever, and His faithfulness to all generations." God is faithful in all things, and He is faithful to those who call on Him for salvation. And so the writer of Hebrews reassures our faith in God when he writes, "²³Let us hold fast the confession of our hope without wavering, for He who promised is faithful."

Paul taught these great truths to the Church at Corinth when he wrote, "⁴I give thanks to my God always for you because of the grace of God that was given you in Christ Jesus, ⁵that in every way you were enriched in Him in all speech and all knowledge—⁶even as the testimony about Christ was confirmed among you—⁷so that you are not lacking in any gift, as you wait for the revealing of our Lord Jesus Christ, ⁸who will sustain you to the end, guiltless in the day of our Lord Jesus Christ. ⁹God is faithful, by whom you were called into the fellowship of His Son, Jesus Christ our Lord" (1 Corinthians 1:4-9). Notice that one of the ways that God preserves His children to the end is through the gifts He gives to the Church. He established His Church for the purpose of teaching and equipping believers so that they would be able to work well for His kingdom and so that they would endure (Ephesians 4:10-16).

9) Those who believe to the end are rewarded with eternal life.

According to God's Word the endurance of believers in always rewarded with eternal life. The writer of the Book of Hebrews puts it this way: "³⁵Therefore do not throw away your confidence, which has great reward. ³⁶For you have need of endurance, so that when you have done the will of God you may receive what is promised. ³⁷For, "Yet a little while, and the coming one will come and will not delay; ³⁸but My righteous one shall live by faith, and if he shrinks back, My soul has no pleasure in him" (Hebrews 10:35-38). Notice that we are commanded to "not throw away [our] confidence, which has great reward." We are commended to have endurance "so that when you have done the will of God you may receive what is promised." And finally he writes that it is not the person who shrinks back from faith that is pleasing to God, but only the one who lives by faith.

It seems to be the understanding of the writer of Hebrews that only those who endure to the end will inherit eternal life. I believe this is because of everything we have talked about up to this point. It is clear that when a person truly comes to Christ with saving faith that He makes them new, gives them His Holy Spirit, and preserves them to the end. Therefore, the writer of Hebrews can state that if we endure we will receive what was promised.

If that is not clear enough, look at the word of Jesus Himself in Mark 13:13, "[13]And you will be hated by all for My name's sake. But the one who endures to the end will be saved." Jesus's statement gives us certainty that He saves the one whose faith makes them to endure. Jesus states this truth again and again in the Book of Revelation in His message to the churches. He states in Revelation 1:10-1, "[10]Be faithful unto death, and I will give you the crown of life. [11]He who has an ear, let him hear what the Spirit says to the churches. The one who conquers will not be hurt by the second death." Jesus even warns the churches in Revelation 3:11, "[11]I am coming soon. Hold fast what you have, so that no none may seize your crown."

It seems throughout Scripture that God rewards the one who endures to the end with eternal life. It does not appear that God is pleased with those who have fallen away permanently.

Conclusion

I think it is important to clarify something as we close out this chapter. It is obvious from all of the Scripture that you have been presented that it is only the believers whose faith endures to the end that will inherit heaven. The point of pointing this out is not to say that I am the judge of whether or not your faith is enduring or legitimate. I know that there are circumstances where people fall into such despair and depression because of life's circumstances and even because of different medicines, and it is not uncommon for those people to take their life. Most ask the question, "Did that person go to heaven?" The answer is that I don't know and neither do you. There is only one God and He does not give us the authority to determine the legitimacy of a person's faith.

The point of this book and this chapter is to help you examine your own faith. My prayer for you as you work through this book is that you ask yourself if your faith is the kind the Bible calls "saving". If you have read this and know that what you thought about being a Christian falls short of what God says it is, please consider coming to Jesus in faith and repentance. Surrender yourself to God in humility, believing that His Son Jesus Christ died for you to absorb the penalty of your sins. Believe that He rewards your faith and repentance with forgiveness and eternal life. Believe that He will always be faithful to you and will make you a new creature created for good works and eternal life.

CHAPTER 6
Discipleship

HOW CAN THE Church of God prevent more people from having a false assurance of eternal life? I am not talking about keeping people from being assured of eternal life; I am talking about keeping people from being falsely assured of something that they do not possess? Remember Jesus told us that "²²On that day many will say to Me, 'Lord, Lord, did we not prophesy in Your name, and cast out demons in Your name, and do many mighty works in Your name?' ²³And then I will declare to them, 'I never knew you; depart form Me, you workers of lawlessness'" (Luke 7:22-23). Notice again that Jesus said that there will be "many" on the Day of Judgment that are falsely convinced that they knew God. So, how can the Church lessen that number of people among them? This is how: We can and must be obedient to the command of Christ to make disciples. That's the answer: *discipleship*.

Discipleship is the process by which a true believer in Christ teaches the Word of God to another person and leads and encourages that person to follow and obey all of the commands of God. Discipleship was expressly commanded by Jesus in the mission that He gave to His Church in Matthew 28:18-20:

"¹⁸And Jesus came and said to them, "All authority in heaven and on earth has been given to Me. ¹⁹Go therefore and make disciples of all nations, baptizing them in the name of the Father and of the Son and of the Holy Spirit, ²⁰teaching them to observe all that I have commanded you. And behold, I am with you always, to the end of the age."

Jesus commanded His Church to "make disciples" and to "teach them to observe" all that He commanded. Jesus did not merely call His Church to *lead people to make "decisions"* or to *lead people in a prayer.* Jesus commanded His Church to make disciples. True followers are what God is after. People who are truly committed to surrendering their lives to Him and committed to striving for obedience to His commands are His desire.

The passage that we have looked at so many times in this book has been Matthew 7:21-23, and in vs.21 Jesus says very clearly that He is looking not for those who call Him "Lord," but those who live as His disciples—those who do the will of the Father. He says, "²Not everyone who says to Me, 'Lord, Lord,' will enter the kingdom of heaven, but the one who does the will of My Father who is in heaven." A disciple is one who follows his teacher. A disciple's chief responsibility is to imitate his teacher. He is like an apprentice who observes, learns from, and emulates his master-teacher. Jesus said, "⁴⁰A disciple is not above his teacher, but everyone when he is fully trained will be like his teacher" (Luke 6:40).

So how do we prevent the number of falsely assured people? We take them through discipleship. We invest in them and make for certain that they know all the commands of Jesus and are willing to follow Him where He promises to take them. It would be a tragedy for someone to spend eternity in Hell when we could have done more to teach them all that Christ commanded and urge them to follow Him.

Three Discipleship Failures

I contend that there are at least three ways that we can fail when it comes to discipleship, or teaching others the commands of God and urging them to follow Him in obedience. The first is that the we sometimes just fail completely to disciple people. The second is that we sometimes fail to disciple people correctly. The third is that we fail to disciple people correctly by our example. We will deal with each of these aspects in turn.

Failure to Disciple (teach)

We fail when we neglect to disciple or teach people the commands of God. We must care for those in whom the seed of the Gospel has been planted. Like a diligent farmer cares for his crops, we must care for those we share the Gospel with and are leading to follow Jesus.

Anyone who has planted a garden successfully knows that you cannot simply plant seeds in the ground and then come back some months later and enjoy the fruit. It just doesn't work like that. A diligent farmer will take the utmost care of his plants, especially when they are young. Often, a person who plants a garden will first plant the seeds in small pots and keep them indoors and out of the early spring frost. He will nurse those plants with just the right amount of water and sunlight and make sure that they stay warm enough while they are young and feeble. As winter's last chilly days are past, and the young plants are strong enough, the farmer will then take them out to plant them in the ground that he has tilled and prepared. That farmer will continue to follow his garden's progress and provide it with the necessary elements to survive and be fruitful. He is a good gardener.

Discipleship works in much the same way. In the Gospels, Jesus compares the Gospel message to a seed, and He compares the hearts of men to soil. The one who preaches the Gospel is like a farmer who is casting out seeds. In Luke 8 Jesus taught a lesson on the Gospel seeds being planted into different kinds of hearts. There's the hardened heart that never even receives the seed and the birds snatch away the good seed that never implants that hard ground. There's the rocky heart, where the seed of the Gospel is unable to take deep roots, and because it has no roots it shrivels up and dies when times of testing comes. There's also the heart that receives the Gospel in a superficial way, but when the plant seems to grow it is choked out and dies as the person cares more for riches and the world than Jesus. Then finally there is the heart of good soil. When the Gospel is planted it receives it and it springs up into a healthy plant and life that bears fruit. The diligent farmer, the one casting the seeds of the Gospel, will be faithful not only to cast the seeds, but also to tend the garden of the heart. If he is determined to help those in whom the seed of the Gospel is planted he will be counted as a faithful disciple-maker.

Much of the teaching in churches about evangelism (sharing your faith with non-believers) is centered on that initial encounter with a person where you tell them about Jesus. Many of us are familiar with what it takes to "share your faith", but many Christians have no idea what it means to disciple that person with whom they are sharing the Gospel. When Jesus commanded us to go into the entire world, He did not command us to only *tell* them about Him. No, He commanded us to *disciple* them and to *teach them all that He commanded.* Obedience to Jesus' command means that we work with those people we share the Gospel with in order to teach them the commands of Jesus. This is what it means to *disciple* them, but so often this never even takes place.

Do we really expect for a person to follow Jesus is they don't even know the commands of Jesus? How is that even possible? How can you obey commands you don't even know? And how will they know if we don't teach them? Discipleship is so much more than just sharing your faith in Christ. Discipleship is a process whereby we commit ourselves to that person, to teach them, lead them, mentor them, encourage them, and help grow them.

The Apostle Paul gave us a wonderful example of what it means to truly *disciple* someone. He spoke of his relationship with the people he discipled in Thessalonica as he said, "[11]For you know how, like a father with his children, [12]we exhorted each one of you and encouraged you and charged you to walk in a manner worthy of God, who calls you into His own kingdom and glory" (1 Thessalonians 2:11). Paul viewed his responsibility to disciple as equal to the responsibility of a parent to his/her child. In fact, in 1 Thessalonians 2:7 Paul characterized his commitment to disciple the Thessalonians "like a nursing mother taking care of her own children." If the Church took on that kind of commitment to teaching people the commands of God and leading them to maturity in the faith, I think that there would surely be less people who were falsely convinced of salvation. As the ones we disciple learn all that Jesus demands of them, it would become apparent to them whether or not they were really committed to Him.

Paul was constantly reminding the Corinthians of the foundations of the Gospel. He was committed to discipling them. He was not going to let any of them be falsely convinced of a salvation that they did not possess. He wrote to them, "¹Now I would remind you, brothers, of the Gospel I preached to you, which you received, in which you stand, ²and by which you are being saved, if you hold fast to the word I preached to you—unless you believed in vain" (1 Corinthians 15:1-2). Paul was committed to discipling people. He was going to make certain that the Corinthians were really committed to Christ for the long haul.

Not only did the Apostle Paul set an example of discipleship for us, but we are clearly told in Scripture that one of the fundamental functions of Church leadership (Elders) is to ensure that the people in the Church are discipled in correct doctrine and protected against false teachings. This is an essential qualification and duty of an Elder (pastor). Titus 1:9 says of an Elder that, "⁹He must hold firm to the trustworthy word as taught, so that he may be able to give instruction in sound doctrine and also to rebuke those who contradict it." The Lord set up His Church for missions and for discipleship. That is clear in the stated purpose in His giving spiritual gifts to His Church. In Ephesians 4:12-14 the Word says that God gave spiritual gifts to the Church "¹²to equip the saints for the work of the ministry, for building up the body of Christ, ¹³until we all attain to the unity of the faith and of the knowledge of the Son of God, to mature manhood, to the measure of the stature of the fullness of Christ, ¹⁴so that we may no longer be children, tossed to and fro by the waves and carried about by every wind of doctrine, by human cunning, by craftiness in deceitful schemes." If we fail to disciple and fail to build up the body of Christ, we fail to obey the commands of God given to us.

Discipleship Failure—When discipleship is a bad thing.

When we understand the definition of discipleship, that it is teaching and leading, it is easy to realize that discipleship can be a very bad thing when what we're teaching is incorrect. We can be the greatest disciple-makers in the entire world, but the question is, "What kind of disciples are we making?" We need to examine *what kind* of disciples we are making and *what kind of doctrine/teachings* we are teaching them.

Jesus pointed out vividly to the Pharisees that they were very good at making the bad kind of disciples. He pronounced a terrifying condemnation on when we stated, "¹⁵Woe to you, scribes and Pharisees, hypocrites! For you travel across sea and land to make a single proselyte, and when he becomes a proselyte, you make him twice as much a child of hell as yourselves" (Matthew 23:15). What a statement! Discipleship is a terrible thing and an absolute failure when we are teaching people to follow commands that Jesus did not give. When we teach and lead people to follow something or someone other than Jesus, the same condemnation falls on us.

Jesus explained to the Pharisees in another condemnation that they were teaching bad things because they believed bad things. He said, "¹³But woe to you, scribes and Pharisees, hypocrites! For you shut the kingdom of heaven in people's faces. For you neither enter yourselves nor allow those who would enter to go in" (Matthew 23:13). The Pharisees' brand of discipleship was no good because they themselves did not believe the right things about Jesus. They didn't believe the right things about God and thus they couldn't teach the right things about God.

When we set out to make disciples of Jesus we must be certain that we are teaching His commands and not our own. We must be certain that our teaching on Him is correct. If we don't we will surely lead someone astray. You must strive to know that you are believing and teaching correctly about Jesus. Wouldn't you be devastated if it was partially your fault that a person was falsely assured that they had eternal life with Christ all because you wrongly assured them with a false teaching?

Discipleship Failure—Bad example.

Discipleship can be an utter failure when we are a bad example to follow. We all know that *actions speak louder than words*. You know that people will follow the example of your life quicker than they will follow your words. The problem is that when the example of our lives is a bad example, people could end up doing the same sinful things that we do.

The Pharisees, like many of us, had a terrible problem with this. Concerning them, Jesus said, "²The scribes and the Pharisees sit on Moses' seat, ³so do and observe whatever they tell you, but not the works they do. For they preach, but do not practice" (Matthew 23:2-3). We can't expect for the people looking to us for spiritual guidance to listen to our words instead of our actions. It's just not natural. If you are a believer in Jesus, you have been commanded to make disciples. But if your example is so poor that you lead people away from Jesus, then you are absolutely failing at being a disciple-maker.

Jesus had nothing good to say about the Pharisees' bad

example. In Matthew 23 He called them "blind guides" twice, "blind fools", "blind men", and "hypocrites!" He called them "hypocrites" because they were telling people to obey the commands of God and to follow God and to love Him, but they weren't doing those things. They weren't loving God with their actions. They were only being religious because they felt like it made them look good and honorable, but Jesus called them "blind" because they couldn't even see the error of their own ways.

The Pharisees were bad examples and hypocrites because they were never really born again. They were never made clean by Christ and changed within. That's why they were making bad disciples. Those disciples were *not following* God just like the Pharisees were *not following* God. They were interested in looking the part of the religious man, but they weren't actually interested in obeying the commands of God and loving Him with every fiber of their being. Discipleship goes terribly wrong when the disciple-maker is not truly saved.

Conclusion

Are you actually a follower of Christ, or do you just want people to think you are? Are you trying to look the part but not are not really transformed within and born again? Jesus called had this to say about those kinds of people: "²⁷Woe to you, scribes and Pharisees, hypocrites! For you are like whitewashed tombs, which outwardly appear beautiful, but within are full of dead people's bones and all uncleanness. ²⁸So you also outwardly appear righteous to others, but within you are full of hypocrisy and lawlessness" (Matthew 23:27-28). If you are not making disciples, could it be because you are failing to teach people the commands of God? Could it be that you are teaching them the wrong things about God? Could it be you yourself don't even believe the right things about God?

Maybe you need to examine your own heart and see if you will contend with Jesus on the Day of Judgment saying, "'Lord, Lord, did we not prophesy in Your name, and cast out demons in Your name, and do many mighty works in Your name?'" only for Him to respond by saying, "I never knew you; depart from Me, you workers of lawlessness" (Matthew 7:22-23).

CHAPTER 7
Keeping the Gospel Difficult

T HERE ARE MANY people in the world today that claim
that they are *Christian*. Claiming to be *Christian* means
many different things to many different people, but the name
"Christian" was first used as slander-calling followers of Jesus,
"Little Christs." People who followed Jesus in the early days
of the Church knew that there would be great difficulties and
persecution if they were to claim the name of Christ, and
so they did not do it *casually* or *to fit in*. They claimed to be
Christian because that is what they were. They embraced the
true Gospel and all the difficulties of following Jesus because
they truly believed.

Being a Christian means much more than claiming that
you *believe* in Jesus. We keep going back to Matthew 7:21-23
in this book because it tells us that on the Day of Judgment
there will be many who name the name of Christ but don't
truly know Him, and we have to ask ourselves, "How did this
happen?". I would contend that we are not *keeping the Gospel
difficult*. I did not say "we are not *making* the Gospel difficult,"

but rather "we are not *keeping* the Gospel difficult." The Gospel is already difficult. Jesus said, "Enter by the narrow gate. For the gate is wide and the way is easy that leads to destruction, and those who enter by it are many. For the gate is narrow and the way is hard that leads to life, and those who find it are few" (Matthew 7:13-14). The Gospel that leads to eternal life, according the Jesus, is "hard" and we don't need to make it hard, we just need to tell the truth and preach the Gospel in all its difficulty.

Modern day church growth movements have led many people and preachers to be "seeker sensitive" and preach a message that is entertaining, pleasing to the ear, and easy to handle. They do this because they feel that they can get more people to follow Jesus, or just join their church, if they make it easy. But that's the problem isn't it? Truly following Jesus is not easy, and to tell someone that "the way that leads to eternal life" is easy, we are lying to them. If someone accepts this false gospel, the "just ask Jesus into your heart" Gospel, then what they become is not a true Christian but rather a false convert. This is the kind of person that will stand before Jesus on the day of their death and tell Him that they knew Him and He will say, "I never knew you" (Matthew 7:23).

There is a technical name for people who claim the title of Christian but don't really know God and it is "nominal Christian." That simply means that they are Christian in name only. Jesus talked about nominal Christians in Matthew 15:8-9 when He described them like this: "This people honors Me with their lips, but their heart is far from Me; in vain do they worship Me, teaching as doctrines the commandments of men." I fear that there are many people who are claiming to be Christians when in fact they are far from God and do not know Him. They are convinced that they do know Jesus because they have believed in a false gospel that does not demand repentance of sin and commitment to holiness.

Jesus never watered down the Gospel. He never made it easy for people to follow Him. In fact, He made it very difficult and always had the same requirements of true faith and repentance of sin. Look at how Jesus dealt with a certain rich man and you will see that Jesus didn't make it easy for him:

> And behold, a man came up to Him, saying, "Teacher, what good deed must I do to have eternal life?" And He said to him, "Why do you ask Me about what is good? There is only One who is good. If you would enter life, keep the commandments." He said to him, "Which ones?" And Jesus said, "You shall not murder, You shall not commit adultery, You shall not steal, You shall not bear false witness, Honor your father and mother, and You shall love your neighbor as yourself." The young man said to Him, "All these I have kept. What do I still lack?" Jesus said to him, "If you would be perfect, go, sell what you possess and give to the poor, and you will have treasure in heaven; and come, follow Me." When the young man heard this he went way sorrowful, for he had great possessions" (Matthew 19:16-22).

This man loved his money more than he loved Jesus. He was convinced of his own goodness and love for God, but the truth was that he was a worshiper of his possessions. Jesus made that clear to him and called him to repent of it by telling him to sell it all. When the man was confronted with the difficulty of following Jesus-the absolute commitment and repentance that Jesus demands-he was unwilling. I have thought for many years that verse 22 is heartbreaking. It says, "When the young man heard this he went way sorrowful, for he had great possessions." The man knew what he was doing. He went away knowing he was walking away from the Christ and it made him sorrowful, but he wasn't willing to turn from everything to follow Jesus. But notice this: the account ends there. Jesus didn't go after the man and soften His demands. Jesus was willing to let the man walk away and He wasn't going to make it easier. Jesus knew that following Him is difficult and He knows that God only saves those who "have no other God before" Him (the first command, Exodus 20:3). Jesus *kept* the Gospel difficult.

This would not happen in many churches today. This man was young and rich, the perfect church member! He seemed to be a decent fellow, and he even sought Jesus out. But he was unwilling to give everything up to follow Jesus. Would this man be told that he had to be willing to walk away from it all today? Would it be made clear that God demands, without exception, to be the only God that you worship? If we are to be faithful to Jesus and His example in preaching the Gospel we have to *keep the Gospel difficult.*

Will there be people who are turned off or turned away when the true demands of Christ are made known? Yes. But that does not make it wrong. Jesus said that there would be few who are saved because the way to eternal life is hard. Listen to His words in Luke 13:23-24, "²And someone said to Him, "Lord, will those who are saved be few?" And He said to them, ²"Strive to enter through the narrow door. For many, I tell you, will seek to enter and will not be able." I think we should be very skeptical about a gospel that is not turning some people off and away. Many people find the demands of the true Gospel offensive, and that should be expected. The

Apostle Paul described the Gospel as offensive to some when he wrote, "We preach Christ crucified, a stumbling block to Jews and folly to Gentiles, but to those who are called, both Jews and Greeks, Christ the power of God and the wisdom of God" (1 Corinthians 1:23-24). If we are preaching a gospel that is pleasing to all, then we are not preaching the Gospel of Jesus. Jesus' Gospel of salvation was offensive to many and great news to some.

Jesus never shied away from the difficulty of the Gospel. In fact, He taught us that we should tell people that He requires everything from those who would seek after Him and the eternal life He gives through the forgiveness of sins. Read this passage of Jesus teaching the crowds and notice how much emphasis He puts on people really counting the cost of following before they decide to or not:

> "Now great crowds accompanied Him, and He turned and said to them, "If anyone come to Me and does not hate His own father and mother and wife and children and brothers and sisters, yes, and even his own life, he cannot be My disciple. Whoever does not bear his own cross and come after Me cannot be My disciple. For which of you, desiring to build a tower, does not first sit down and count the cost, whether he has enough to complete it? Otherwise, when he has laid a foundation and is not able to finish, all who see it begin to mock him, saying, 'This man began to build and was not able to finish.' Or what king, going out to encounter another king in war, will not sit down first and deliberate whether he is able with ten thousand to meet him who comes against him with twenty thousand? And if not, while the other is yet a great way off, he sends a delegation

and asks for terms of peace. So therefore, any one of you who does not renounce all that he has cannot be My disciple" (Luke 14:25-33).

Unless you are willing to leave it all, then you are not willing to give all that Jesus requires of you. For us to tell anyone any different is deceitful and hurtful in the most profound way. What good does it do anyone to believe a false gospel and spend eternity in hell? Does anyone honestly think that it is permissible to teach a gospel contrary to the one that Jesus taught? Is it really alright for a church to boost their attendance, membership, and giving by watering down the demands of God? By no means!

Jesus never lessened the requirements of following Him. Those passages you read are not abnormal to the message of Jesus. Those passages you read are the consistent message that He preached, and who is man to change that? Again, look at how plain Jesus made it that the way to eternal life is difficult:

"As they were going along the road, someone said to Him, "I will follow You wherever you go." And Jesus said to him, "Foxes have holes, and birds of the air have nests, but the Son of Man has nowhere to lay His head." To another He said, "Follow Me." But he said, "Lord, let me first go and bury my father." And Jesus said to him, "Leave the dead to bury their own dead. But as for you, go and proclaim the kingdom of God." Yet another said, "I will follow You, Lord, but let me first say farewell to those at my home." Jesus said to him, "No one who puts his hand to the plow and looks back is fit for the kingdom of God" (Luke 9:57-62).

Jesus demands that those who follow after Him actually *follow* after Him! And He doesn't leave any doubt about it. He actually tells them that if they aren't willing to leave everything and follow Him as the Lord that they were not "fit for the kingdom of God." We would serve our fellow man well to tell them the whole truth and present them with the undiluted Gospel. If we don't tell them the things that Jesus demands, it is likely they will name the name of Christ, but it is unlikely that they will do what Jesus commanded them. Friend, we cannot afford to do that to people. Don't we understand that eternity is at stake? Don't we believe that Hell is a real place that real people will endure for eternity without the Savior? If we do believe that, then preach the Gospel and don't water it down! Call people to follow after Jesus with all their heart and all their soul and all their strength, not holding anything back. Anyone who comes to Christ unwilling to leave all to follow Him is not fit!

We need to remember that we are the preachers of the Gospel, not the writers. We do not have the authority to alter the message or water it down. If we do alter the message, we risk producing false converts, which means that they are still dead in their sin, bearing all the weight of the legal demands of their sin, and headed for an eternity in Hell (Colossians 3:13-14).

The Church must fight the temptation to produce *decisions for Christ* at the expense of the message. We must fight the temptation to produce greater attendance numbers at the cost of preaching a watered-down gospel, which is indeed a false gospel. Churches, Christian Summer Camps, and Conferences take great pride in *numbers*, but they must not seek the numbers to the point of altering the message. We must be faithful to Jesus by preaching the Gospel at full strength,

AUTHENTIC FAITH

with all of the demands of God. We need to remember that
the promise of salvation is only for those who will *leave it all*
and follow after Jesus (Luke 14:33).

Conclusion

I understand that when we preach the Gospel in all its
difficulties that many people will be turned off and turned
away by their own refusal to surrender completely to Christ.
But we can't afford to preach any other way. We need to trust
God that He will indeed save people and grant them faith to
surrender completely to Him. As it is, we know Jesus said,
"No one can come to Me unless the Father who sent Me
draws him. And I will raise him up on the last day" (John
6:44). It truly is a miraculous work of God when someone
becomes willing to leave it all and surrender to Christ. Again,
Jesus said, "It is the Spirit who gives life; the flesh is no help
at all. The words that I have spoken to you are spirit and life"
(John 6:63).

Is it difficult for someone to leave their old life behind
to follow Jesus? Yes. Is it difficult for someone to turn from
worshiping their possessions and embrace Jesus? Yes. When
you begin to think about these difficulties remember the
words of Jesus to His disciples:

> "And Jesus said to His disciples, "Truly, I say to you, only
> with difficulty will a rich person enter the kingdom of
> heaven. Again I tell you, it is easier for a camel to go
> through the eye of a needle than for a rich person to
> enter the kingdom of God." When the disciples heard
> this, they were greatly astonished, saying, "Who then
> can be saved?" But Jesus looked at them and said, "With

man this is impossible, but with God all things are possible" (Matthew 19:23-26).

God is able and willing to save people. Jesus wants us to preach the unaltered, full-strength Gospel and trust Him through faith to save people. Church, don't base your value and worth on *decisions*. Base your value and worth on your faithfulness to God and to preach the Biblical Gospel. After all, only the true Gospel will lead to true salvation.

www.ingramcontent.com/pod-product-compliance
Lightning Source LLC
Chambersburg PA
CBHW030854090426
42737CB00009B/1224